FLEXIBILITY FOR S\

FLEXIBILITY FOR SWIMMING

Paddy Garratt

Kaye & Ward · London

TO PAT

Who always **meant** to exercise!

First published by Kaye & Ward Ltd
Century House, Tanner Street, London SE1
1980

ISBN 0 7182 1274 6

Printed in Great Britain by
The Pitman Press, Bath

CONTENTS

Introduction

It has been obvious over the years that the greatest swimmers have been very flexible. Swimmers such as Mark Spitz, Roland Matthes, Shane Gould, Cornelia Ender, David Wilkie and John Naber all displayed in and out of the water the loose limbed and lithe look which we now come to expect of a world champion.

Is it coincidence that the best swimmers all seem to have 'sabre' legs (legs which bend the **wrong** way at the knees?) No, of course it is not, it is in fact an asset to them when performing their art, just as the full range of flexibility in their shoulders particularly when performing backstroke and butterfly is an asset to them.

Is it not then reasonable to expect that to improve one's performance in the water it would be in one's interest to try to mould one's physique as near as possible to that of the proven masters, even if their flexibility is so obviously natural? After all we try to improve our strength and our technique in the hope that we may emulate the world-class performer, why not our flexibility?

Why Do We Require Flexibility?

Firstly, in order to get the best advantage out of the swimmer's physique when performing a particular stroke. The swimmer needs to be able to get the fullest range of movement possible from the joints controlling the limbs used.

It follows that in order to get the fullest range of movement possible from the swimmer's limbs, the joints are required to be as flexible as possible, thus enabling the swimmer to reach, lift or hold the most advantageous limb positions throughout the stroke without causing undue stress to any particular joint.

To give two very simple examples of this:

a) The swimmer needs to be able to extend the arms in front of the body, either singly or both at the same time as in front crawl or breast-stroke without there being any undue stress in the shoulder joint and muscles surrounding it.

b) The swimmer needs to be able to lift the elbow high in the recovery of butterfly and front crawl, again without any undue stress to the shoulder joint.

It should be remembered that if we cannot reach an advanced level of flexibility, it is going to be rather difficult to obtain a good relaxed position within the stroke.

In many cases swimmers only need to work at their flexibility exercises in order to maintain their natural flexibility, but the majority must work hard just to improve their poor range of movement.

Overall Flexibility and Mobility Work

Many swimmers tend to think of flexibility as just stretching the shoulder joints and in the case of breast-strokers, the knees. We must study the body as a whole. An agile, flexible, lithe body will lend itself to the flowing and undulating movements through the water. Consider the overall mobility required to perform the latest starting dive techniques, the most efficient turns and the undulation of a top-class butterfly stroke, the high arching of a well-executed backstroke start. Water-polo players with their fast twisting bobbing and weaving movements and synchro swimmers with their aquatic gymnastics all need the overall mobility exercises of the neck and spine.

Not only do the body exercises improve overall mobility but they also stimulate and in some cases massage the internal organs of the stomach. They improve the circulation and at the same time help the swimmer to be more aware of body control.

A top-class swimmer needs the rhythm of a dancer, the grace and agility of a gymnast, the reactions and power of a track athlete, all of whom practise a great deal of flexibility work in their training.

Swimming Muscles

The ideal swimming muscles are required to be long, slim and powerful. Therefore swimmers who indulge in weight training or any other kind of strengthening work need to do a balanced amount of stretching to stop the muscles from 'bulking' as they gain in strength, which in itself will hinder the movements of the shoulder joints in particular.

Long, slim, powerful muscles will also ensure strength throughout the full range of the propulsive movements. This surely is good enough reason for making flexibility a part of one's training programme.

I am of the opinion that no weight training programme should ever be undertaken without an equal and alternative flexibility programme. This will not only stop any injury occurring, but it will also maintain the natural fexibility of the young swimmer in later years.

My approach is to do a forty-five minute weight training session, alternating daily with a forty-five minute flexibility session. This method will ensure that as well as gaining strength, the muscles will maintain the length, slimness and elasticity so important in swimming.

Swimming Injuries

Next we consider the stress which the surrounding ligaments of the joints undergo in certain strokes. If we examine our joints, we will quickly realise that some of them are severely restricted in their actual movement. Take for instance the knee and elbow joint. They are both only designed to bend one way, plus a certain amount of rotation. On the other hand the shoulder, hip, ankle, and wrist joints have multiple movement, as do the many individual joints of the spine. The very restricted joints such as the knee and elbow are prevented from moving from side to side by very strong ligaments. These ligaments come under a great deal of pressure when certain strokes are performed, i.e. breast-stroke (knee), backstroke (elbow), because of the force which is exerted on the inside of the leg or arm in each case. Not only are the ligaments being stretched under a great deal of pressure, but the joint is undergoing a rotating movement at the same time. These two combined movements can in some cases, cause inflammation to the restricting ligaments and surrounding tissues. The symptoms are commonly known as breast-stroker's knee and backstroker's elbow.

Few problems are experienced with the hip joints as far as pain is concerned. Unfortunately the same cannot be said of the shoulder joint which in recent years has become a very real problem, with many world-class swimmers experiencing a great deal of pain due to the massive distances undertaken in training. The main problem here is that pain is felt due to the continued abrasive movements of the main ligaments and tendons of the shoulder against the various bone endings which make up the shoulder joint. The medical term for this complaint is tendonitis which is inflammation of the tendons or ligaments and surrounding tissues. It is not at all surprising that the pain which I described becomes evident when one considers the amount of use a shoulder gets during a heavy training session. In a normal balanced programme, a top competitive swimmer could well complete in excess of 10,000 circular movements of each shoulder joint in a week. It is not difficult to imagine the wear and tear which the joint must undergo. Therefore it must make sense that the more flexible, loose, mobile and relaxed we can make the shoulders during this time, the less likely they are to become damaged. These problems can be avoided if regular continuous flexibility exercises are performed from an early age.

Recognising Injuries

I have been using flexibilty and mobility exercises for several years now, and have found that my swimmers experience very few muscular and joint problems which a couple of days' rest will not overcome. This is so even though they are on a year round three sessions per week weight training programme.

At the first sign of an underlying pain which is usually situated quite deep in the front of the shoulder or on the inside of the knee, the swimmer should be kept out of the water and completely rested for at least two days. On no account should he or she be encouraged or allowed to carry on training.

This pain should not be confused with normal 'training soreness', which is a result of the commencement of heavy water work or weight training.

What is the Difference between the Two Types of Pain?

Normal 'training soreness' will be felt over the whole muscle surface. A general soreness will be felt when the limbs are moved and the muscles will feel tender to the touch all over. The soreness is attributed to the lactic acid build-up in the newly-worked muscles and usually will disperse very quickly when exercised again. A good session of flexibility work will aid the dispersal and soothe the soreness.

'Training Injury pain' is a completely different matter and should be treated very differently. This pain will be felt in an isolated area, which can be pinpointed by gently probing with the fingers deeply into the affected area and can usually be traced back to the muscle ending. However, the pain does sometimes radiate from the injured area (for instance a tendon in the shoulder joint) down the arm giving a dull and very uncomfortable pain which is often described by swimmers as 'toothache in the arm'. This is the danger signal and it seems to me that only immediate rest will have any effect on this type of injury. After two to three days' rest or maybe even a week, a series of gentle flexibility exercises will tell if it is cured or on the mend.

I felt it important to cover the subject of injury in this chapter in order to clear up any confusion regarding the types of soreness. I am, however, convinced that if a swimmer completes a good all-round session of flexibility work at least every other day from the commencement of competitive training, he or she will never experience either of these two types of soreness.

Flexibility Before Competition

A selection of free standing, floor and passive resistance exercises should be completed before commencing the competition warm-up. Not as many as one would use in a normal flexibility session, but at least a good selection from each group. This will aid our warm-up considerably and help the loosening-up process in this age of overcrowded warm-up sessions.

In many cases, we find that by the time the swimmer gets round to competing, one or two hours may well have passed since the initial warm-up, rendering it virtually useless. In such cases it is very necessary to complete a selection of free standing exercises while waiting to be called to the starting block during the preceding race.

British swimmers are renowned for their slow moving, quiet, almost bored approach to even the most important races. I am convinced that they would benefit a great deal from a short, sharp, vigorous session of free standing exercises while waiting at the blocks. If, for no other reasons but to get active and mobile, to increase the pulse rate somewhat and to sharpen the reflexes.

Flexibility and Stretching as an alternative to 'Swimming Down'

It is of course a well known fact that 'swimming down' or 'compensatory swims' during or after training are a most important aid to recovery. In doing so they remove the metabolic waste (carbons, lactic acid, lymph fluid etc.) from in and around the muscles.The removal of these waste products is necessary in order that our specific methods of training, whether in or out of the water, may operate to maximum effect on our muscular system.

Flexibility and stretching exercises have very much the same effect on the muscles as a 'swim down' or 'compensatory swim' and will aid recovery in the same way. Therefore a good selection of exercises should be performed at the conclusion of training as well as at the beginning, whether in the 'weight room' or the pool.

Each group of muscles exercised during weight training should also be stretched throughout the session.

On finishing a competitive swim **when a 'swim down' is impossible** a series of stretching and flexibility exercises should be undertaken, **as soon as possible** after leaving the water.

TIME SPENT STRETCHING GROUPS OF MUSCLES WILL NEVER BE TIME WASTED.

Relaxation During and After Flexibility Work

To get the best out of each exercise, it is necessary to develop one's ability to relax. When the fullest extent of stretching is reached in each exercise, then a very positive attempt should be made at relaxing the muscles round the particular joint being exercised. This period should be held for approximately five seconds. This may seem to be rather a difficult thing to do as in most cases the whole joint, including the surrounding muscles, is under tension but with practice, a great deal of relaxation can be achieved.

At the completion of a full flexibility session, I recommend five to ten minutes of total relaxation and meditation in a sitting position with legs crossed in front, the body in an upright position with the spine straight from seat to head. The arms should rest on the knees with the index fingers touching the thumbs.

When this position has been obtained, then the mind should take over from the body. Think of total relaxation, the whole weight of the body going through the floor. Face muscles relaxed, back muscles, arm muscles, hip, thigh and calf muscles all should now be relaxed and thoughts should turn to pleasant things, a mental calmness. The calmness must cover the whole body, let go and drift in this state, away from the stresses of competition and training.

These very special minutes of relaxation will most likely be the only time a swimmer will be able to completely relax in any given day — as each is timetabled in order to get the most out of it. The hectic daily routine of training, school, homework leaves very little time for relaxation so take advantage of this time. It will also give the swimmer a feeling of wellbeing after completing what should be a mildly demanding session.

Discipline

I must stress at this point the importance of complete and utter discipline when working with a group. The exercises must be carried out correctly and in good style in complete silence. The only sound that should be heard is the word 'stop' when the passive resistance work is being carried out and the full extent of the exercise has been reached. The operator needs to know how far to go and a great deal of damage may be caused if they do not hear the word 'stop' murmured gently by the subject.

During the whole of a flexibility session, an air of calm and quiet should prevail during all exercises. Swimmers not prepared to co-operate should be asked to leave the group until such a time when they are mentally ready for such discipline.

Group Work

Providing the correct discipline is maintained, it is possible to work with as many as forty or more swimmers in a group. The best method is to have the group in a circle, with the coach in the inside where he can observe every swimmer with ease. Ideally when teaching the group the movements and positions, the coach should either demonstrate the positions to the group by example or with a swimmer who is experienced in the work. The demonstration, with or without a swimmer, should be well rehearsed beforehand so that the group will be able to understand how many of the movements 'flow' into each other.

The safety factor of the partner work should be well covered in the initial stages and **never** allowed to deteriorate under any circumstances.

Obviously in a climate such as ours, most of the year's work will be indoors but whenever possible, try to get outdoors to do your exercises where you may at the same time take advantage of the fresh air and sunshine, most important to the development and growth of young bodies.

Flexibility and Planning Your Programme

With so many muscles, tendons and ligaments originating from or lying near the joints, particularly the shoulders it is impossible to say which particular exercises are most important in avoiding pain, loosening the overall joint, or improving muscular elasticity. There are many areas of potential problems, therefore we need to cover as many exercises as possible in each session. Up to as many as thirty exercises plus a warm-up run can be fitted into a well organised forty-five minute session.

It is necessary to get the whole body as warm or even as hot as possible before undertaking the following exercises. Probably the best and certainly the quickest way is by running (which in itself is a valuable training aid) either on the spot or over a short course. A distance of one to one-and-a-half miles will suffice. The running should preferably be done on grass or inside a gymnasium but never on the road or on a concrete surface, as this will without doubt cause injuries to a swimmer's ankles or knees. Another substitute for running when space is not available are 'step ups' which will very quickly raise the temperature of the body to the level necessary before the exercises should be executed.

As I have implied in the previous chapters, the reasons for doing flexibility and mobility exercises are numerous, both in avoiding pain, keeping the muscles' length, increasing the range of joint movement, and providing an aid to recovery.

I have attempted to include as many exercises as possible, designed to increase or maintain overall flexibility throughout the body. The large number of exercises will enable the swimmer or coach to plan a schedule all the year round and still be able to 'ring the changes' so that boredom does not set in. This surely is the key to keeping the training programme interesting.

FREE STANDING EXERCISES

Warm-up Exercises
for shoulders, pelvis, joints and general stretching of allied muscle groups

The whole group doing the 'free standing' exercises.

Before commencing the following exercises, time should be spent on arm circling forwards and backwards approximately twenty-five times each way. Brush the ears with the arms as they pass the head.

EXERCISE 1

(a) Palms together, stretch.

(b) Keeping palms together, bend elbows until the thumbs touch spine between shoulder blades. The whole of the lower arms should be pressed close together, and head lifted back as far as possible. Hold for five seconds.

(a)

(b)

EXERCISE 2

(a) Place left foot sideways on, while extending right leg back and in line with left foot. Bend front knee until thigh is parallel to floor and rest left hand palm on the floor.

(b) Stretch right arm out in advance of the head and aim at getting a straight line from foot to finger-tips.
Repeat on opposite sides.

(a)

(b)

EXERCISE 3

(a) Right arm extended up and straight, left arm straight down to side.

(b) Drop right hand behind head to middle of back. At the same time, lift left hand up to meet right hand.

(c) Pull up with right hand, pull down with left hand alternately. Hold each position for count of five.
In one continuous smooth unhurried movement, change arms. Repeat.

(a)

(b)

(c)

EXERCISE 4

(a) Stretch arms above and behind head. Cross wrists and grip fingers together.

(b) Without releasing grip, swing hands forward and down.

(c) Hold position with elbows as close together as possible for approximately five seconds. Repeat several times.

(a)

(b)

(c)

EXERCISE 5

(a) Crouch down on balls of feet with heels touching, knees apart, fingers touching the ground, back straight and erect. Extend one leg to the side. Lock knee straight, ankle extended, toes pointed.

(b) Hold position for five seconds. Change position smoothly until legs are in opposite positions. Repeat several times.

(a)

(b)

EXERCISE 6

(a) Stand with feet together, body erect. Extend arms up above and behind the head. Relax each joint, wrist, elbow, shoulder, hips, knees, ankles. Stretch! Grow in height! Repeat several times. Feel that you are growing taller.

(b) Reach back, as far back as possible to end this stretching exercise. At the same time, push head forward.

(a)

(b)

(a)

(b)

EXERCISE 7

(a) In the standing position, reach up with right arm as high as possible.

(b) Drop hand down behind back. Touch spine with middle finger, reaching down as far as possible.

(c) Grip right elbow with left hand.

(d) Pull right elbow behind head as far across centre line as possible. Hold for five - ten seconds. Repeat whole exercise with opposite arm.

(c)

(d)

EXERCISE 8

(a) Stand with back erect. Right foot fifty centimetres in advance of left. Entwine fingers of both hands behind back. Lift as high as possible up back by bending elbows.

(b) Bend forward at the hips. Touch right knee with chin, forehead or nose. Knees must remain straight at all times. Hands must remain together, with elbows in the bent position.

(c) With one smooth movement, extend arms until elbows are completely straight. Press hands in direction of the ground in front of you for five seconds. Complete exercise again with left foot in front.

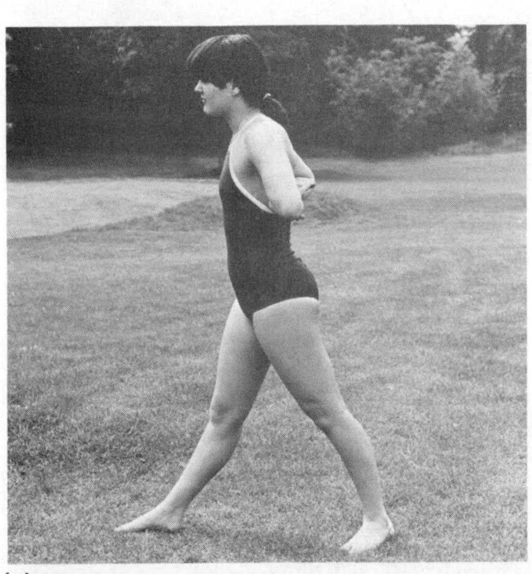

(a)

(b)

(c)

(a)

(b)

EXERCISE 9

(a) Stand erect with feet together, arms extended, palms facing down.

(b) Swing arms back with a smooth relaxed, but firm motion to the count of three, increasing the backward pressure on each count. The hands must remain at the same level as the shoulders throughout the whole exercise. Repeat at least four sets. Relax arms down to sides at the end of each set, i.e. after each count of three.

(c) The aim is to eventually touch hands behind back on third press while at the same time keeping hands at shoulder level.

(d) Repeat all above with palms of the hand upwards.

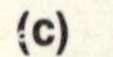

(c)

(d)

EXERCISE 10

(a) Step forward with right leg extended into a comfortable stance. With body in upright position stand with arms out to the side on a level with the shoulders.

(b) With one smooth movement, lean forward and twist at the hips bringing the back of the left arm against the side of the right leg. Hold position for count of ten. Complete whole exercise in opposite direction.

(a)

(b)

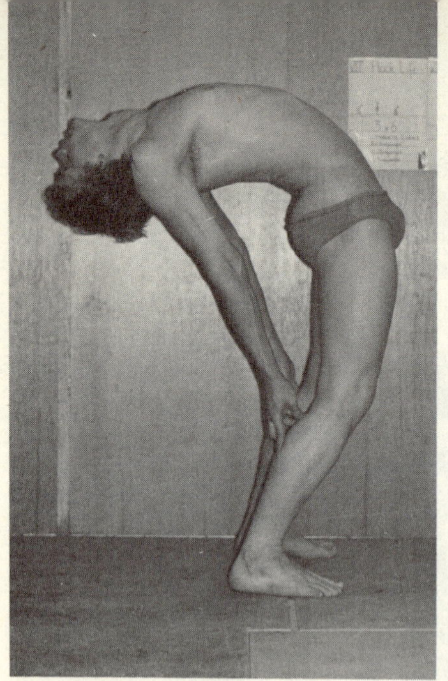

(a)

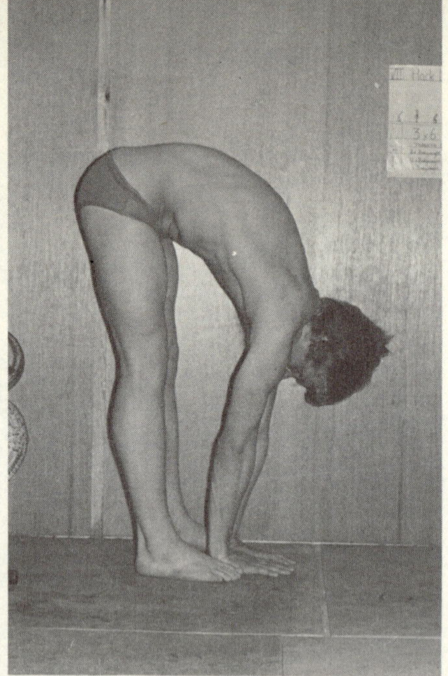

(b)

EXERCISE 11

(a) Stand with hands touching back of the thighs, feet slightly apart. Slide hands down the back of the legs, at the same time lean back as far as possible. Try to look at the floor behind you. Hold maximum bend for five seconds.

(b) From last position stand up straight, move slowly into the hands flat on the floor position. Make sure that the knees are kept straight.

(c) From last position grip ankles, point elbows out to the side, pull head as close into the knees as possible.

(c)

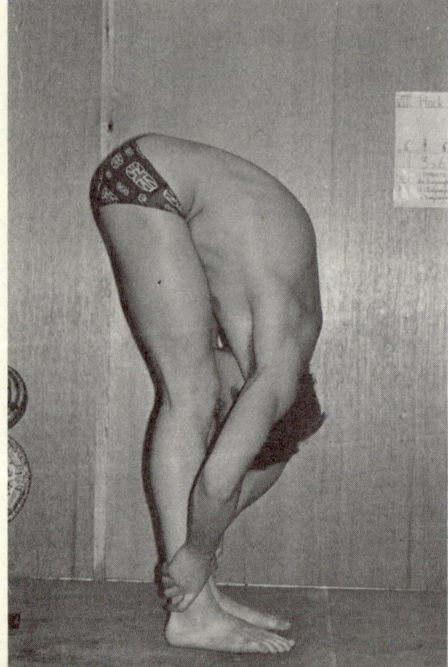

EXERCISE 12

(a) Lean forward with fingers interlocked behind back. Keep the body at a forty-five degree angle to the legs. Lift the arms up and forward with elbows straight as far as possible.

(b) From the last position, stand up straight. At the same time release hand grip. Take up thumbs locked position in front of the legs, lift arms up and back smoothly, as far as possible with elbows straight.

(a)

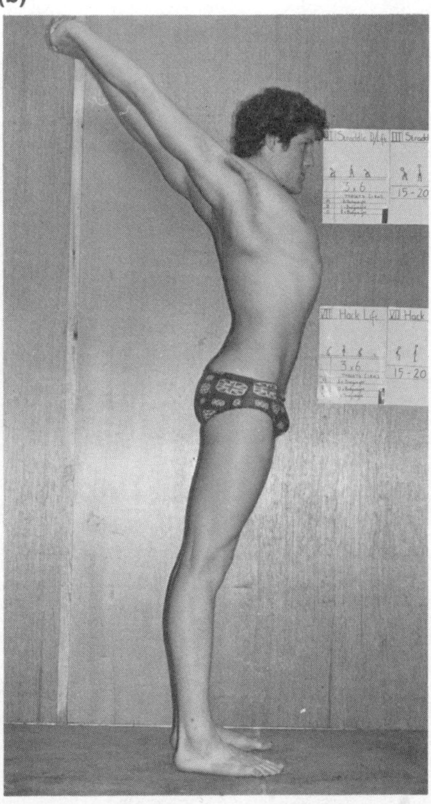

(b)

FLOOR EXERCISES

for hips, spine, ankle, shoulder joints and the stretching of allied joint and muscle groups

A controlled group performing floor exercises with the author supervising.

EXERCISE 13

(a) Kneeling in an upright position. Grip ankles with thumbs on the inside. Slowly lift hips in a forward position, at the same time dropping the head back.

(b) Complete exercise by fully arching the back. Hold for ten seconds.

(a)

(b)

EXERCISE 14

(a) Lying on the front in a completely relaxed manner, place a marker approximately seven centimetres in advance of the fingers. In turn relax and stretch, relax and stretch again until the marker is reached.

(b) In some cases it is possible to increase the distance between the marker and fingers as much as twelve centimetres.

(a)

(b)

EXERCISE 15

From the last exercise in the fully stretched position, walk slowly and smoothly backwards with the hands into a seal-like position. At the same time lift the head back as far as possible. Holding the completed back arch for ten seconds.

EXERCISE 16

(a) Lying on the front in the manner described in exercise 14(a), slowly lift feet and arms off the ground.
Slowly bring the hands and feet together with the knees bent.

(b) Grip the ankles with the hands. Push back with the feet. Pull the front of the body up with the hands.

(c) Hold the completed position with the feet and hands as high as possible for ten seconds.

(a)

(b)

(c)

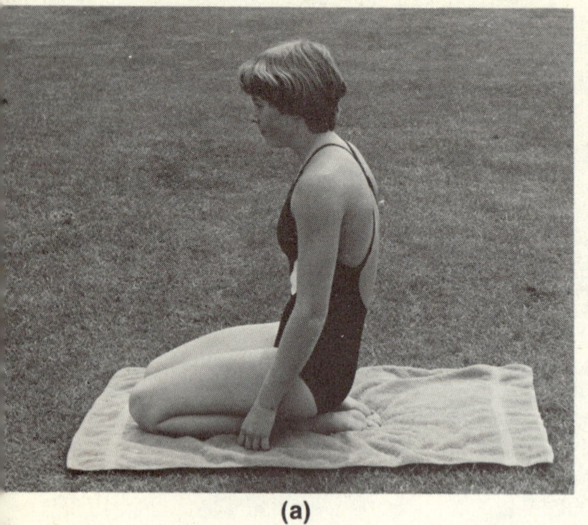

(a)

(b)

EXERCISE 17

(a) Kneel with the feet and knees touching, while sitting on the heels.

(b) Lean back, support the body with the arms, hold for ten seconds.

(c) Lower the body down on to the elbows, hold position for ten seconds.

(d) Complete the exercise by lowering the body until the shoulders are on the ground, arms out to the side.
Hold final position for fifteen seconds as relaxed as possible.
Complete the sequence in reverse until you are in the upright position.

(c)

(d)

EXERCISE 18

Sitting upright, pull feet as close to the body as possible. Soles of the feet together, place hands on to the knees. With a gentle but firm bouncing movement press the knees down as close to the ground as possible.

EXERCISE 19

(a) Sitting in an upright position, hands on the ground with arms straight in support, place the left foot on the opposite side of the right thigh above the knee.

(b) Bend the right knee until the heel is touching the left buttock.

(c) Twist the shoulders and head as far round to the left as possible. Place the right arm with elbow locked against the outside of the left knee. Grip the left ankle with the right hand using the arm as a lever against the knee to increase the twisting position to its maximum. Hold for fifteen seconds. Return to front sitting position.

Repeat complete exercise to the opposite side.

(a)

(b)

(c)

EXERCISE 20

(a) Sitting in the upright position, place the right ankle underneath the left knee.

(b) Extend the arms forward, gripping the left ankle firmly with both hands.

(c) Lift the elbows as high as possible. Pull against the ankle as hard as possible, pressing the head down to touch the left knee. Hold final position for fifteen seconds.
Return to sitting position. Repeat exercise with the opposite ankle under the opposite knee.

(a)

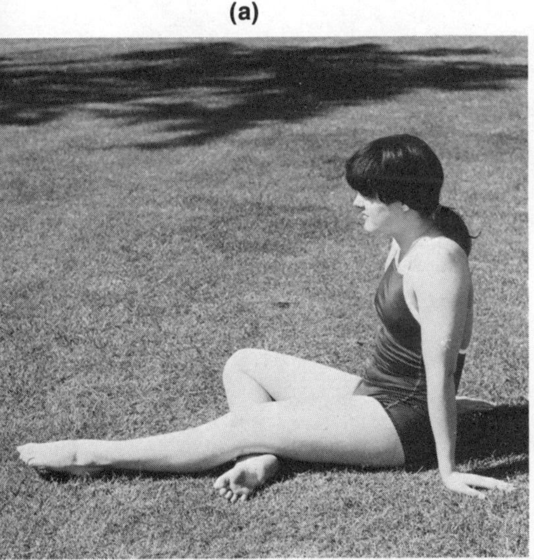

(b)

(c)

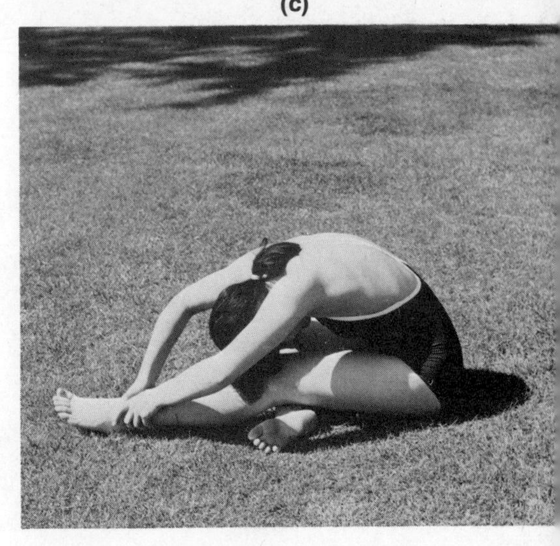

EXERCISE 21

(a) Sitting with the legs approximately one metre apart, grip ankles.

(b) Lift the elbows as high as possible at the same time lean as far forward as possible. Pull the head down attempting to touch the ground. Hold for fifteen seconds.

(a)

(b)

(c) In the same sitting position but with legs approximately forty-five centimetres apart, hold the soles of the feet with the back of the hands facing each other, feet turned inwards, lift elbows as high as possible, lean forward at the same time pulling with the hands. Attempt to touch the ground with the head. Hold for fifteen seconds.

(d) With the legs as far apart as possible, lean forward, reach as far forward as possible with the hands attempting to touch the ground with the head. This exercise should be repeated with clenched fists and with fingers extended. Hold each forward movement for at least five seconds.

(c)

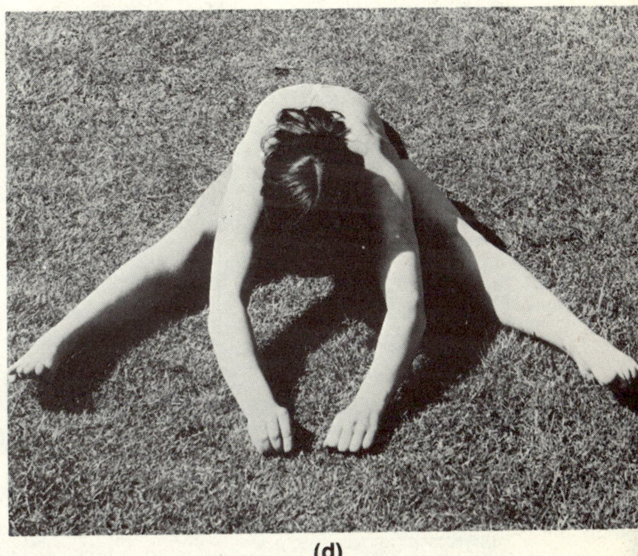

(d)

EXERCISE 22

Sitting in a comfortable position, legs together, supporting body with the hands, extend the feet, try to touch the ground with the toes. Repeat two or three times and hold for approximately five seconds.

EXERCISE 23

(a) Lying face down, grip the right foot at the same time turning it outwards. Press gently down towards the ground. Repeat with the left foot, holding final position for approximately five seconds.

(b) Repeat last exercise with both feet at the same time.

(a)

(b)

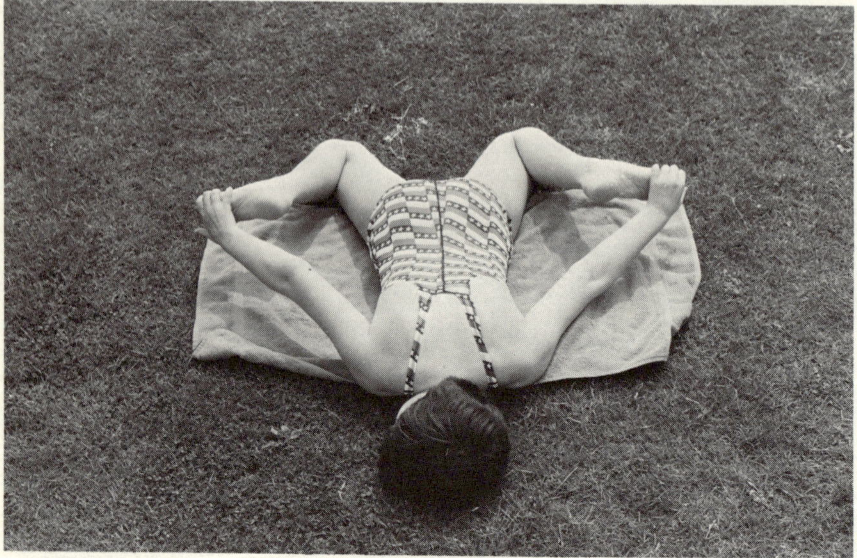

(a)

(b)

EXERCISE 24

(a) Kneeling with the knees five or six centimetres apart, feet turned outwards, inside of the feet flat on the ground, hold position for five seconds.

(b) Sit down between the feet, support the body with the hands. Hold position for five seconds.

(c) Lean further back, support the body on the elbows. Hold position for five seconds.

(d) Lying on the back, arms spread out, shoulders flat. Hold the position for fifteen seconds.

(c)

(d)

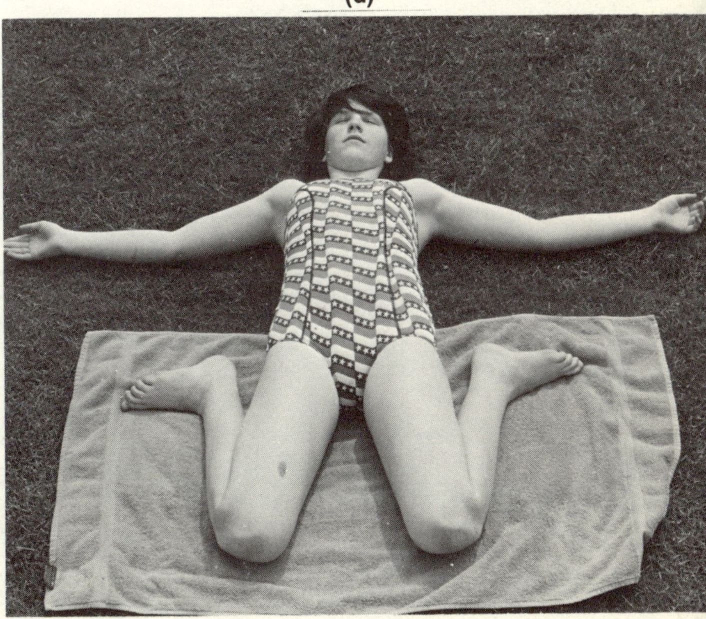

(a)

(b)

EXERCISE 25

(a) Lying flat on the back. Arms straight to the side of the body. Lift the legs into a position 90° to the body.

(b) Supporting the back with the hands, lift the body up until it is being supported as high as possible on the shoulders and upper arms.

(c) Straighten arms when balanced position is gained. Place palms of the hands flat on the ground.

(e)

(f)

(c)

(d)

(d) Keeping the knees straight, touch the ground with the toes on each foot alternately in smooth slow movements.
Return to straight upright postion each time.

(e) Repeat with alternate legs ten times.

(f) Return to straight balanced position. Slowly lower both legs together until toes on both feet touch the ground.
Keep knees straight, hold position for fifteen seconds.

(g) Return to straight balanced position, slowly lower body to the ground in a controlled manner.

(g)

EXERCISE 26

(a) Lie on the back with legs together in the raised position, arms spread out with palms flat on the ground.

(b) Lower the legs slowly to the left until they touch the ground at the side, keep the knees straight throughout. The shoulders should be in as close contact with the ground as possible.

(c) Repeat to the right in the same manner, repeat several times.

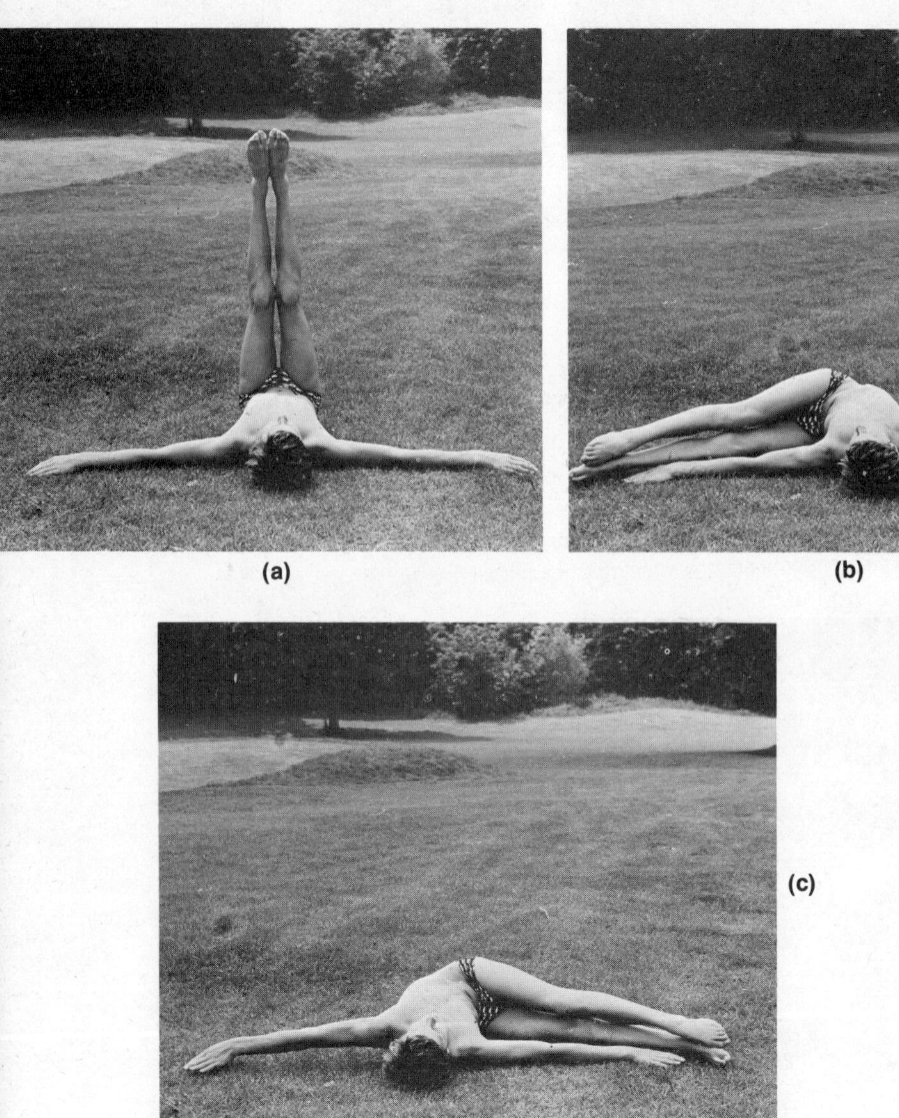

(a)

(b)

(c)

EXERCISE 27

(a) Still on the back, place palms of the hands at the side of the head with fingers pointing towards the shoulders.

(b) Draw the feet up to the seat into a firm comfortable postion.

(c) In one smooth, combined movement, lift the body by straightening the elbows and knees at the same time arching the back as high as possible. Hold the position for ten seconds. Lower the body slowly to the ground in a controlled manner. Do not collapse.

(a)

(b)

(c)

EXERCISE 28

(a) As with exercise 25(a) lift the body into the upright position on shoulders in a straight line from toes to neck in a balanced position, arms extending backwards with palms flat on the ground for support.

(b) Slowly lower the knees to the ground, hold the position for ten seconds in a relaxed manner. Straighten legs and hips, slowly lower body to the ground.

(a) **(b)**

EXERCISE 29

Sitting close to a wall, lean forward with knees bent for support, lift hands as far up the wall as possible with the palms flat against the wall. Raise the body and sit up in an upright position applying gentle but firm pressure against the arms, hold position for ten seconds.

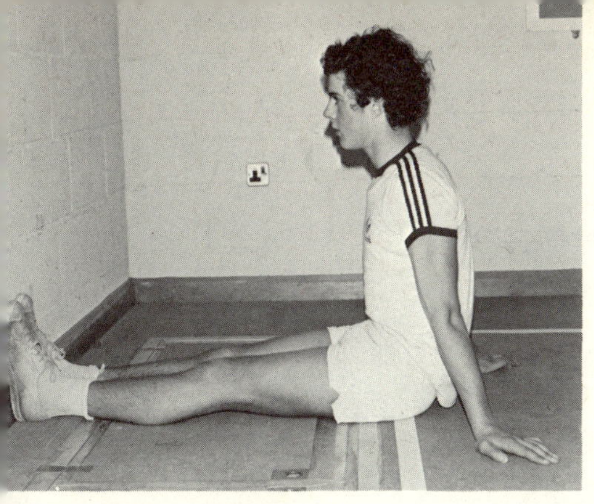

(a)

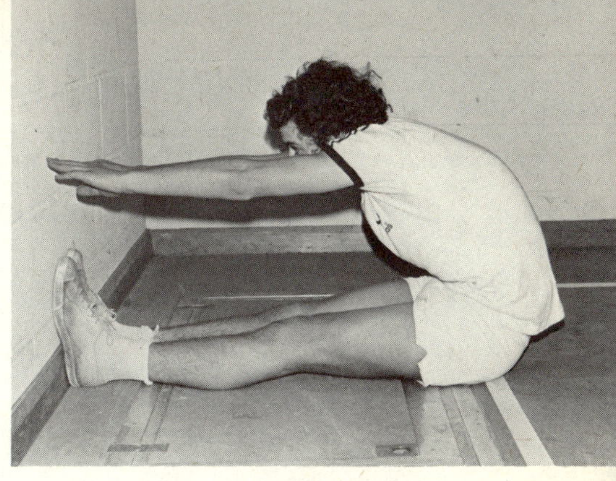

(b)

EXERCISE 30

(a) Sitting upright, feet flat against the wall, knees straight, hands flat on the floor.

(b) Swing both hands forward, touch the wall with finger-tips, clench fists and palms of the hands in turn.

(c) Swing arms back, slide palms of the hands along the floor as far as possible behind the body. Repeat several times.

(d) Repeat complete exercise with hands reaching progressively further up the wall and further behind the body.

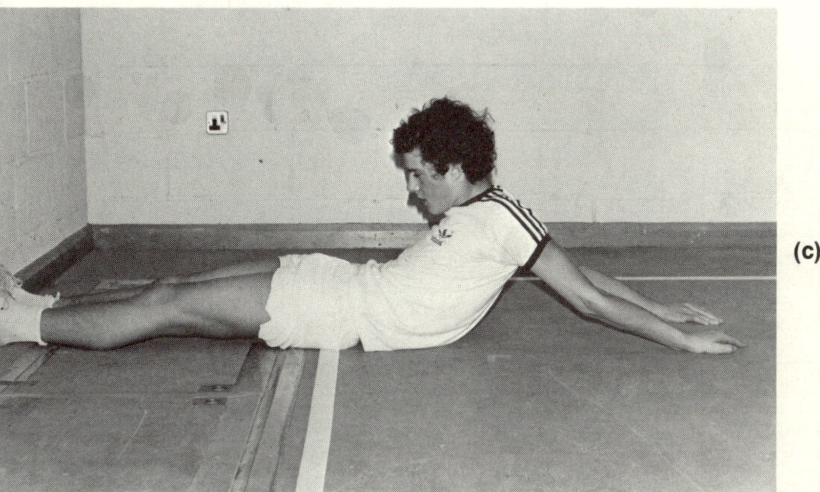

(c)

(d)

EXERCISE 31

(a) Lying flat on the back, bend right knee up to chest and pull in tight to body. Grip ankle and at the same time pull in as tight as possible also. Repeat several times alternatively left and right legs.

(b) Repeat using both legs at the same time.

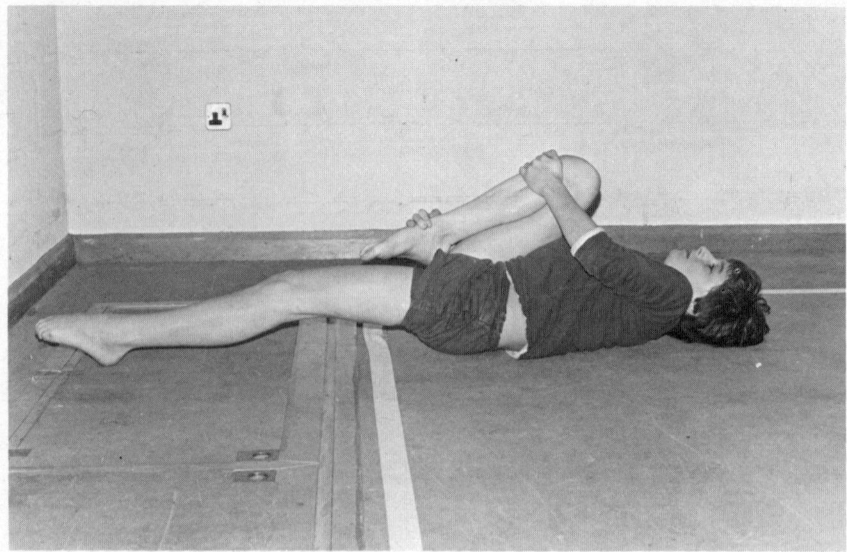

(a)

(b)

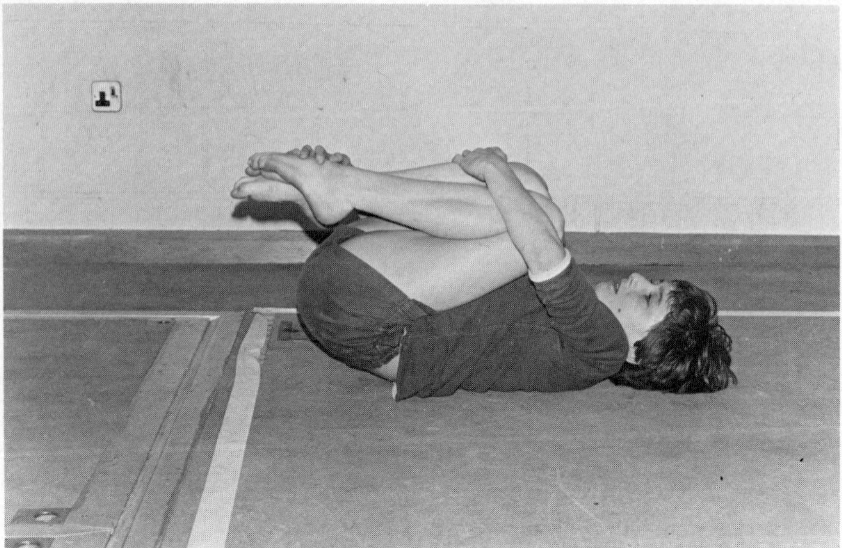

PASSIVE RESISTANCE EXERCISES mainly for the improvement of flexibility in the shoulder joints and the stretching of the allied muscles

Care should be taken in the performing of these exercises that they should never be allowed to develop into a game to see how far the partner can go after complaining of pain.

When the fullest extent of each exercise is reached, release pressure gently.

A period of at least ten seconds should be allowed between each exercise in order that the joint can find its natural position.

Before proceeding with the following exercise, a period of arm circling should take place twenty or thirty times forward and backwards.

A group being led through a series of passive resistance exercises.

(a) (b)

EXERCISE 32

(a) Standing behind subject with the subject in the kneeling position, sitting on the heels, hold partner's wrists. 'Lift' as high as possible as if attempting to lift off the ground.

(b) Cross the arms until the elbows are crossed, slowly slide hands down to the elbows.

(c) Maintain pressure until partner signals 'STOP'. Hold this position for five seconds. Repeat exercise crossing the wrists in the opposite manner, i.e. right over left and then left over right.

(c)

The following shoulder exercises should be executed so that they flow into each other, thus flexing the joints and stretching the muscles through all possible movements and positions.

EXERCISE 33

Partner holds the wrists, turning them outwards (which will keep the elbows locked). Gently apply pressure bringing the back of the hands together or as close as they will go until the subject signals. The arms should be angled in such a way that the muscle tension can be felt. The ideal position is *between* the straight up position and the horizontal position. Hold final position for five seconds.

EXERCISE 34

(a) Partner holds wrists in the same manner, with the arms horizontal to the ground. The back of the hands should be brought together.

(b) As the flexibility increases it will become possible for the arms to cross completely. Hold position for five seconds. Repeat whole exercise with the opposite arm crossing over the top.

(a)

(b)

ADVANCED PASSIVE RESISTANCE WORK

I have mentioned in a previous chapter that when the fullest range has been reached in any one exercise the subject should relax (even though the muscles are under a great deal of tension) and that the partner should hold the final position for approximately five seconds. This particular phase of the exercise can be taken a stage further but only in the case of a subject having undergone passive resistance work regularly for a period of not less than twelve months and even then this next stage should be approached extremely cautiously.

On reaching the fullest range 'STOP' the subject should resist firmly and exert his or her fullest strength against the partner's effort. This action will ensure that the muscles are fully stretched in every aspect of their structure. This effort should be held for five seconds approximately.

EXERCISE 35

In the standing position, partner grips wrists crossing arms behind the subject as close to the back as possible. Increase pressure until subject signals. Hold position for five seconds. Repeat whole exercise crossing the arms in the opposite manner.

EXERCISE 36

Subject kneels on the floor, head tucked well into knees and grips hands together behind back, elbows straight. Raise arms up and over to their fullest extent, partner gently but firmly increases the position until stop signal is given. Hold position for five seconds. Release gently.

The next set of exercises as with the previous set should also flow into each other. Both partners are in the kneeling position.

EXERCISE 37

Place the hands comfortably on the back of the head, fingers extending down the back of the neck. Partner gently but firmly applies pressure to bring the subject's elbows as close together as possible. Release gently.

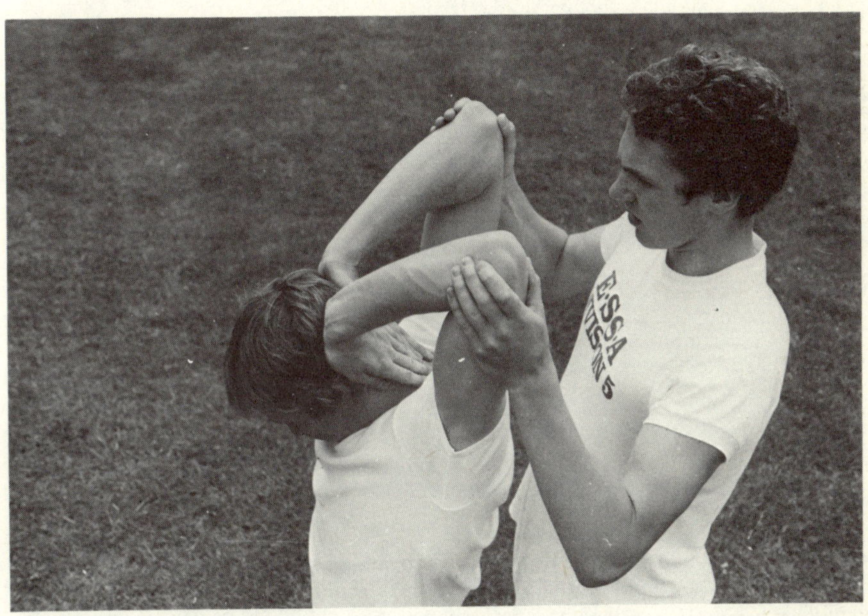

EXERCISE 38

Repeat Exercise 37 with hands resting on upper neck, fingers extending upwards onto the head.

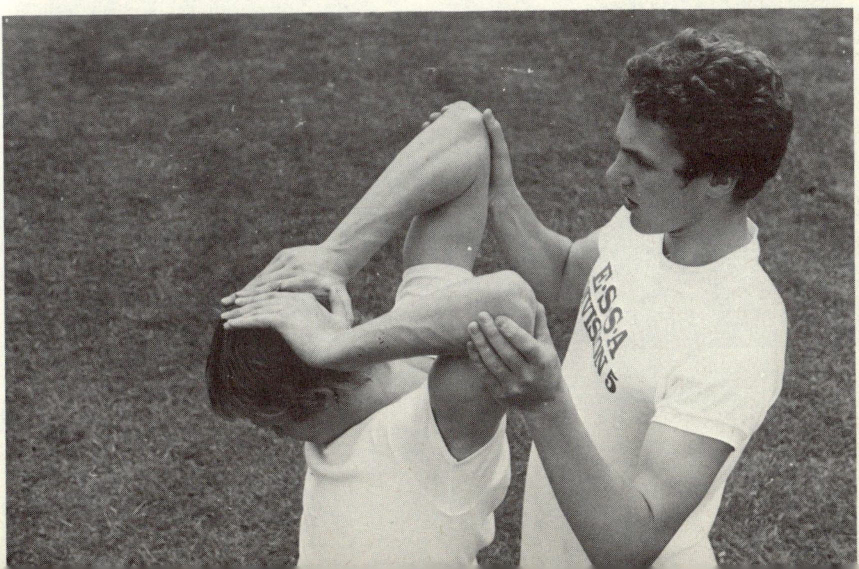

EXERCISE 39

Repeat as for the previous two exercises with the subject placing back of the hands resting against the sides of the face, fingers extended under the chin.

EXERCISE 40

Partners kneel facing each other, subject rests back of the wrists on hips. Partner applies pressure to bring elbows as close together as possible. Hold final position after being given stop signal for five seconds. Release gently.

(a)

(b)

EXERCISE 41

(a) Partners stand back to back, subject raises arms, locking thumbs together, elbows straight. Partner grips subject's arms just above the elbows.

(b) Partner places seat under the subject's seat, leaning forward until subject's back is resting comfortably against partner's back.

(c) Partner firmly exerts pressure against subject's arms, leaning forward to take full weight of subject and lifting subject's feet off the ground. Hold position in a balanced and comfortable manner, apply further pressure to subject's arms until stop signal is given. Gently lower subject to the ground.

(c)

(a)

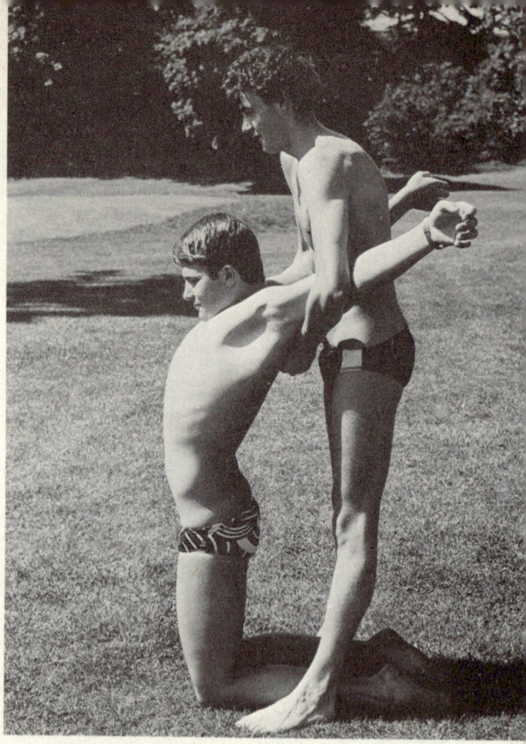

(b)

EXERCISE 42

In some cases it may be found that the partner is not strong enough to exert sufficient pressure against subject's limbs in order to reach the maximum flexibility. Photographs 42(a), (b), (c) show methods of using the whole of the partner's arms to exert maximum pressure.

(c)

EXERCISE 43

A final loosening of the shoulders can be done as shown. Subject lies on the floor, partner grips wrist of subject. The arm should be completely relaxed and moved freely in the shoulder joints. Partner gently moves arms backwards and forwards, side to side and in a circular action clockwise and anticlockwise, until subject feels that shoulders are completely relaxed and loose.

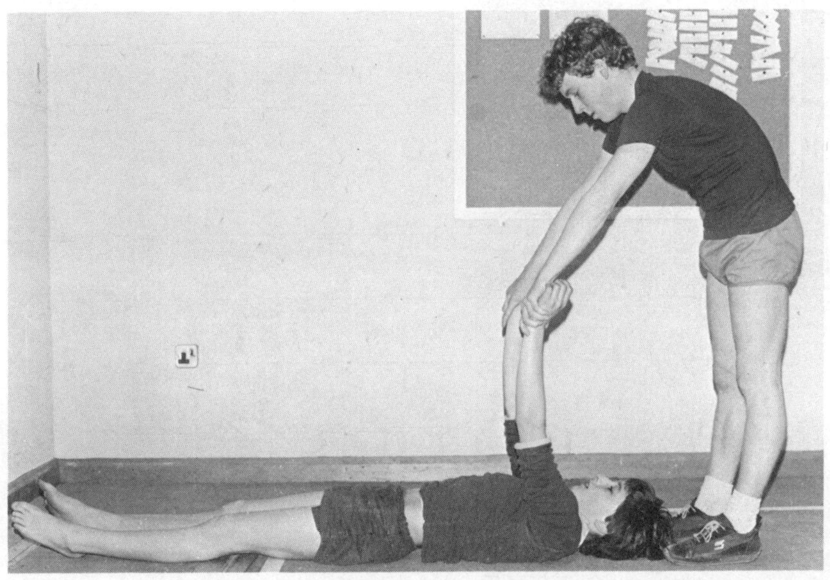

At the conclusion of the passive resistance exercises, another series of arm circling will be beneficial twenty-thirty times forward and repeat backwards, remember to brush the ears with the arms as they pass the head.

General Exercises

The following four photographs show the extent of flexibility that can be reached by performing a regular and controlled programme of exercises as set out in the previous pages of this book.

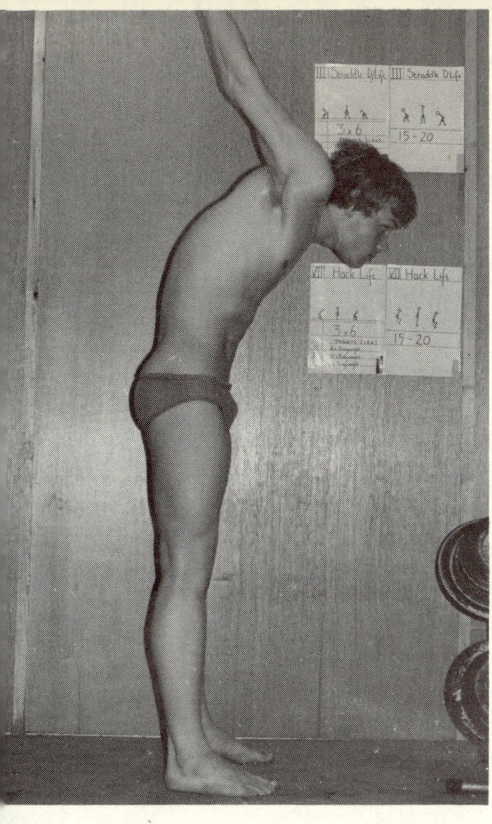

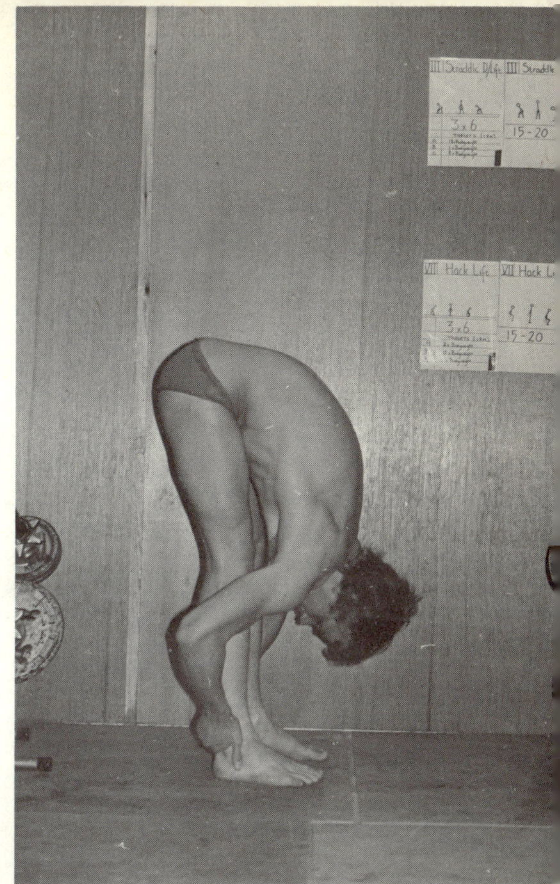

These four swimmers show what is to some extent the natural flexibility of the knees (sabre legs) of National Standard Swimmers. This of course will be improved by executing some of the floor exercises which involve pressure against the muscles on the back of the legs. This flexibility will of course increase the range of kicking movement during backstroke, front crawl and butterfly, thus emphasising the desirable whipping action of the legs.

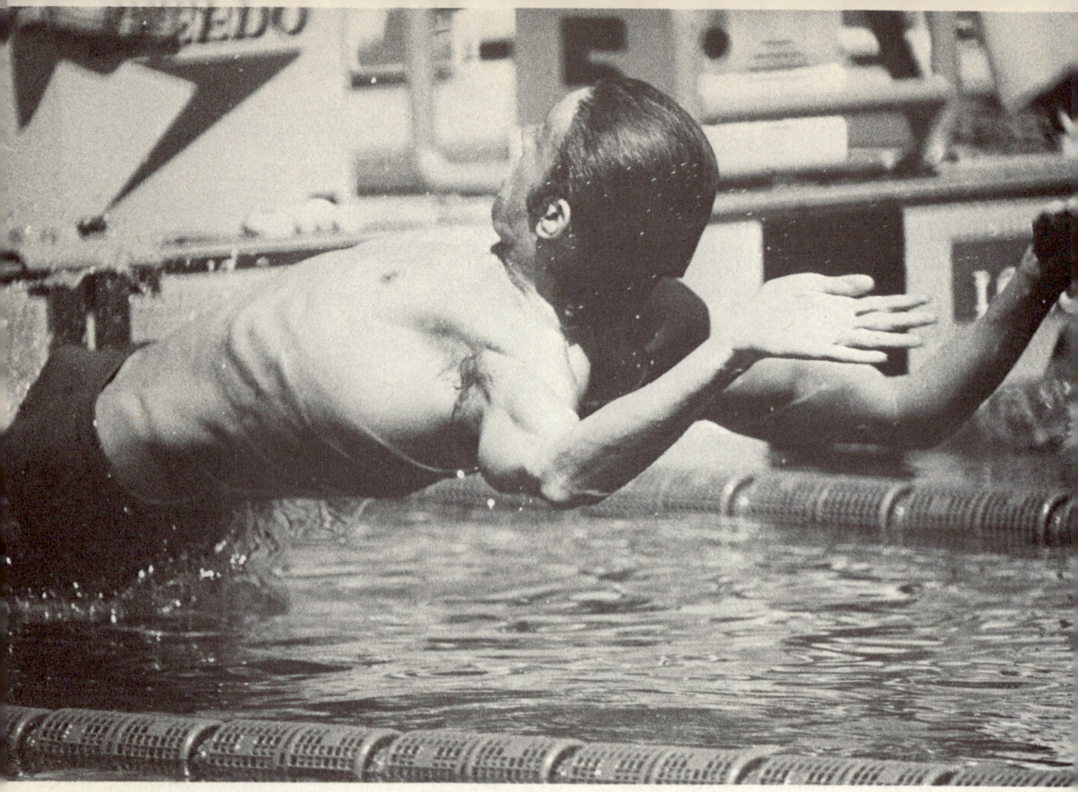

Roland Matthes, G.D.R.
He held world 100 and 200 backstroke records from 1967 to 1973. Showing the extent of his shoulder flexibility while in action. (Photograph by Tony Duffy).

Paul Marshall, G.B.
British 100 backstroke record holder, putting himself through his own particular form of stretching exercise. (Photograph by Ernest Collinson).

Margaret Kelly, O.B.E., G.B. British and Commonwealth record holder for the 100 metres breast-stroke and British Women's Olympic Team Captain, makes ready by stretching.

Duncan Goodhew, G.B., Olympic Gold Medalist.
An ex-pupil of the author. British record holder for 100 metres breast-stroke and Men's Captain to the British Olympic Team, stretching and flexing before the 100 metres Olympic Trial.

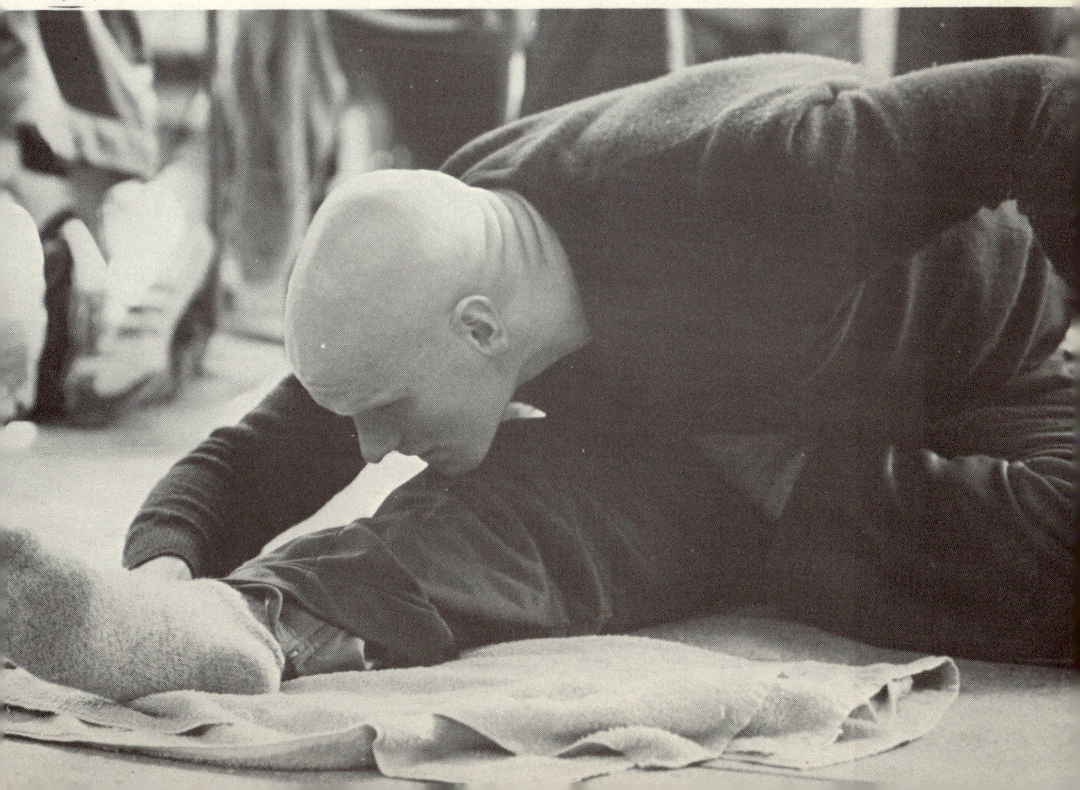

The group at the conclusion of a flexibility session, practising relaxation.

Pop Mobility

'Pop Mobility' is a method of combining stretching and flexibility exercises with 'Pop' Music. It can be great fun, providing it is well controlled and the exercises flow into each other.

Many of the free standing and floor exercises depicted in the previous pages of this book can be adapted to this particular form of exercise with a little imagination.

Any form of popular music can be used, providing it has a good solid beat to which each exercise or part of exercise should be repeated three or four times in time to the beat of the music.

Slower types of music can be used when performing the types of exercise which require a longer stretching phase.

It is not recommended that a complete record of three minutes or so is used, but rather one minute at a time is played, of the chorus, or most popular part of the tune.

This form of performing mobility and flexibility exercise is probably most suited to the synchronised swimmer, but in my experience even the most hardened competitive swimmers have thoroughly enjoyed the odd session of 'Pop Mobility' and have even found it pleasantly taxing and challenging.

More information on this type of exercise can be obtained from:

Mr Ken Woolcott
24 Pasture Road
Wembley
MIDDLESEX 4AO 3JL.

Conclusion

It would be virtually impossible for me to cover every possible known exercise relating to flexibility and mobility in a book of this nature.

What I have done is to try to explain and illustrate a selected number of well-tried exercises in each category, which can be knitted together in order to produce good all-round flexibility and also to cover enough exercises in order that the coach or the swimmer can develop a series of sessions without having to repeat the same exercises day in and day out.

If the reader wishes to develop more exercises, I recommend that they should look into the many excellent yoga manuals on the market today one such is *Yoga for the Athlete* by Harvey Day. Many of the exercises found within these manuals can be adapted to the needs of the swimmer, diver, water polo player and synchronised swimmer.

I sincerely hope that the reader gains as much enjoyment, benefit, and well-being experienced by many of my swimmers present and past.